W9-CCE-351

Sir Humphrey's Honeystands

Written by Christopher A. Lane
Illustrated by Sharon Dahl

A SonFlower Book

VICTOR BOOKS®

A DIVISION OF SCRIPTURE PRESS PUBLICATIONS INC.
USA CANADA ENGLAND

*Dedicated
to my wife, Melodie.
The love of my life.*

KIDDERMINSTER KINGDOM TALES
*King Leonard's Celebration
Sir Humphrey's Honeystands
Nicholas and His Neighbors
Cornelius T. Mouse and Sons*

Scripture quotations are from the *Holy Bible, New International Version,* © 1973, 1978, 1984. International Bible Society. Used by permission of Zondervan Bible Publishers.

1 2 3 4 5 6 7 8 9 10 Printing/Year 94 93 92 91 90

ISBN: 0-897693-845-X

© 1990 SP Publications, Inc. All rights reserved.

VICTOR BOOKS
A division of SP Publications, Inc.
Wheaton, Illinois 60187

Sir Humphrey's Honeystands

There was once a bear who lived in a beautiful house deep in the forest in the Kingdom of Kidderminster. His name was Humphrey and he was very wealthy. In fact, he had so much money that he was a true millionbear. His spacious home resembled a castle, with many large rooms and wide windows. He had servants to prepare his dinner and to clean up after him. He even had servants to draw his bath and lay out his clothes. He lived a kingly life, and the woodland creatures actually considered him a royal bear, of sorts, and called him Sir Humphrey.

He had gotten rich after he had found an enormous beehive. He had sold the honey from it, and the woodland creatures couldn't seem to get enough of it. They thought it a delightful topping for ice cream, waffles, and peanut butter sandwiches. Some took to adding it to their hot tea, while others poured it onto their crumpets and raisin cakes. Still others enjoyed it plain, all by itself.

Humphrey soon found himself swamped with so many orders for honey that he couldn't keep up. He looked for other animals to help him with his honey business.

Freddie the Fox was one of the first animals to come forward. Freddie was a clever sort and seemed very willing to help. Before long, Freddie became Humphrey's chief fox and number-one servant.

Now, years after discovering the beehive, Sir Humphrey had a number of honeystands scattered throughout the forest. He had many servants who took care of supplying honey to the forest folk, and Freddie the Fox was in charge of them all. This left Sir Humphrey free to spend his days relaxing in his spacious manor, sipping tea and eating freshly baked muffins and honey.

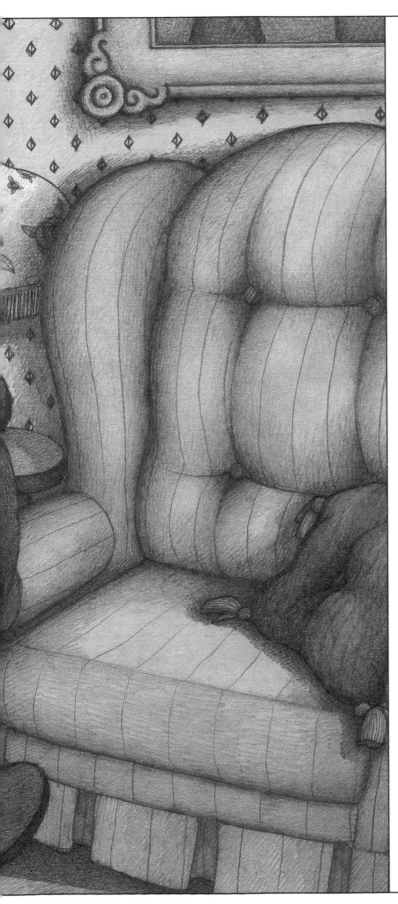

Now it came about one day, just before naptime, that Edward, the bookkeeping beaver, was in Sir Humphrey's study checking the honey records.

"Are my honeystands doing well?" Sir Humphrey asked.

"Oh, yes, quite well," Edward assured him, adjusting his round spectacles. "In fact, you could say . . . hmmm."

"What is it?" Sir Humphrey asked, sitting forward in his tall padded chair.

"Probably nothing," Edward said. "Just a slight . . . discrepancy."

"A slight what?" Sir Humphrey asked.

"A discrepancy— a small problem," Edward explained. "The numbers here don't seem to add up correctly. It seems that one of your servants has— um— 'borrowed' several jars of your honey and failed to return them or to pay you."

Sir Humphrey was silent for a moment, his nose wrinkled up as he wondered what this meant. "One of my trusted servants?" he asked finally.

"Yes, sir. According to these figures, he owes you . . . 99 jars."

"99 jars!?" Humphrey shouted in disbelief.

"No, excuse me. I was mistaken. Let me check these numbers again."

"Whew! For a moment there, I was getting very concerned," Sir Humphrey smiled.

"He owes you exactly 100 jars," Edward announced.

"100 jars!!?" Sir Humphrey nearly fell from his seat. "What on earth could anyone do with 100 jars of honey?"

Edward shook his head. "I have no idea, sir. But I certainly advise you to find out."

"Oh, I assure you, Ed, I will find out at once! Reginald!!!" he roared.

Moments later a regal-looking hound appeared in a clean, sharp butler's uniform. "You rang, Sir Humphrey?" he asked without blinking his sleepy eyes.

"Yes, Reginald, please summon—" Sir Humphrey paused. "Ed, what was the name of that servant?"

Edward flipped quickly through his papers. "It is Mr. Freddie the Fox."

Humphrey started. "Freddie? Surely you are mistaken."

Edward looked down at his documents and then shrugged his shoulders. "It's no mistake, sir," he said. "Freddie the Fox owes you honey."

"Unthinkable. Reginald, have Mr. Fox brought to me at once!"

"Very good, sir. Will there be anything else? A cup of tea before your nap perhaps?"

"No, Reginald. I am too upset for tea or even a nap today."

Reginald nodded and left the room with Edward the bookkeeper. Sir Humphrey sat for some time, staring out the window at the smooth, green east lawn. There were birds hopping about, the sunlight was streaming down through the tall evergreens, and a group of young squirrels were tossing acorns to and fro. But Sir Humphrey did not notice; he simply sat slouched in his chair, muttering to himself.

Finally he heard a knock at the door of his study. "Come in," he said in a deep voice.

Reginald the butler held the door open. "A Mr. Fox to see you, sir."

"Send him in. And have Ed my bookkeeper come in as well."

"Good day, Sir Humphrey," Freddie said brightly as he entered the study. "You're lookin' good, sir. Must be the muffins and honey, eh? Oh, it's awful nice of you to have me over like this. What did you want to talk about? You gonna open another honeystand? I tell ya, I have some ideas about that. I was thinkin' 'bout a place over by the elk lodge. And I—"

"That's not why I've asked you here, Freddie," Sir Humphrey interrupted. "Sit down and listen. Ed, tell Mr. Fox what you found in the records."

"According to these figures, Mr. Fox, you owe Sir Humphrey 100 jars of honey."

Sir Humphrey leaned forward toward the seated fox. "How do you explain this debt?"

"I . . . ah . . . " Freddie stuttered.

"Well," Sir Humphrey asked, "did you take 100 jars?"

"I guess so," Freddie said quietly.

"You guess so!?" Sir Humphrey roared. "Freddie, whatever did you do with 100 jars of honey? That's enough honey to hold an all-forest pancake feed! We could invite King Leonard and his court, besides!"

"Yeah, I guess you're right," Freddie said.

"What happened to it?"

"I took some home for my family. You remember my family— Lucy, the wife—" He pulled out a wallet filled with photographs. "And there's Dora, our littlest fox. That's Ted, and the tall one is Stan. Boy, are they ever growing."

Sir Humphrey stared intently at Freddie. "Your family couldn't possibly eat that much honey!"

"Um . . . well . . . No, we didn't eat it all. I kind of took some—" his voice sank to a whisper— "outside the forest. And I sold it."

"Where is the money, Freddie?"

"I sort of lost it."

Sir Humphrey gave a long sigh. "What do you mean, you lost it?" he asked, trying not to lose his temper.

"Well, I have this weakness for the ponies, you know, racehorses. I bet it at the racetrack. I thought maybe I could make a little easy money."

"Gambling is never easy money, Mr. Fox," Edward admonished, "especially when you are using someone else's."

Sir Humphrey sank into his tall padded chair. "Let me get this straight, Freddie. You stole my honey, sold it without my permission, and gambled away the profits?"

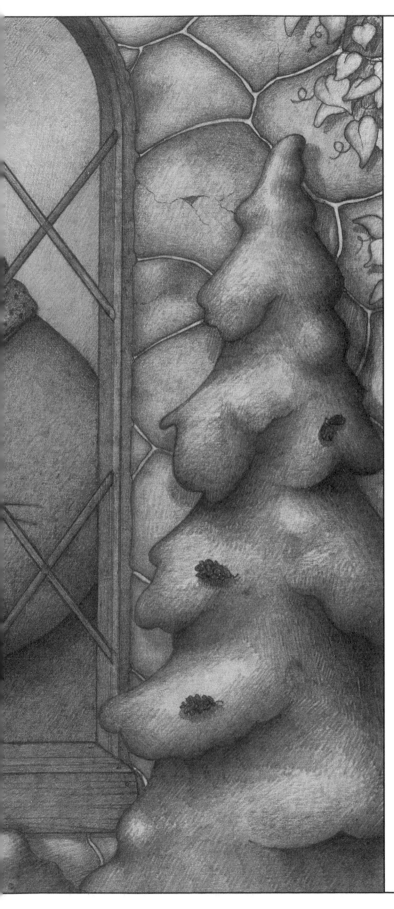

"That about says it," the fox agreed. "I'll pay you back, though. Don't worry. Just give me a little time."

Sir Humphrey rose. "You will pay me back immediately! If you must, sell everything you own."

"But, sir," Freddie pleaded, "you can't mean that. What about my family? How will we live?"

"You should have thought about that before you took my honey."

"Oh, please, sir," Freddie whined, falling to his knees before the wealthy bear. "Please, Sir Humphrey, give me one more chance. You are such a kind, forgiving bear. I really am sorry, sir. What I did was wrong, I know that. Please forgive me. I've learned my lesson. If you'll only be patient with me, I'll pay you back, every single jar. Please, sir . . . "

"Oh, get up," Sir Humphrey said, taking his seat again. "I should have you thrown into jail, but I can see that you are sorry for what you did. I forgive you."

"Oh, thank you, sir!" Freddie cried. "I'll start paying you back as soon as—"

"You could never repay it all," the wealthy bear said, shaking his head. "Ed, strike out his debt."

"Sir?" the bookkeeper questioned.

"Cancel it. Give him a fresh start." Rising again, Sir Humphrey offered the fox his paw.

"Oh, Sir Humphrey, thank you, thank you," the overjoyed fox said. "I'll never forget your generosity and kindness. Thank you!"

"Now back to work with you," Sir Humphrey motioned, "you crazy fox."

"Yes, sir! Oh, thank you, thank you!" Freddie continued, bowing his way out of the room.

Later that same day, an elderly mole dressed in worn, tattered clothing approached one of Sir Humphrey's honeystands. His name was Barnabas, and he was a poor mole who could only afford to buy very small amounts of honey at a time. On this occasion, Barnabas had no money at all, yet he was quite hungry. He stood to the side until the other customers had left.

"Good day, Mrs. Rabbit," the elderly mole said timidly.

"Why, hello there, Barnabas," the rabbit clerk answered cheerily. "I haven't seen you around lately. What can I do for you today?"

"I— I was wondering," he said hesitantly, "if I might have a bit of honey, a small cup perhaps?"

"Of course," she said. Lowering her voice, she said, "Would you like me to put it on your bill?"

"Oh, yes, please, if it's not too much trouble."

Mrs. Rabbit hopped over to the honey bin, dipped out a generous cupful of the sticky golden nectar, and handed it over the counter to the hungry, waiting mole. She wrote down "one cup" on a bill as Barnabas slowly started home.

Just then Freddie the Fox arrived. He visited each honeystand every day to check up on the employees and to make sure that the business was running smoothly.

"Good day, Mr. Fox," Mrs. Rabbit said.

"Don't just stand there, Mrs. Rabbit, get me today's records. Hop! Hop!"

"Yes, sir," she said, scurrying to gather the needed papers. "Here you are, sir."

"Mmmm . . . " he grunted, looking them over. "Very well. I'll be back tomorrow."

Freddie the Fox turned to leave, and walked right into Barnabas, who had stopped to sample the delicious syrup.

"Oh, excuse me, sir," Barnabas apologized as his honey spilled over onto the ground.

"You old fool!" Freddie hissed, wiping droplets of honey from his smooth, shiny coat. Suddenly Freddie recognized the mole. "Hey, aren't you Barnabas? Let's see your money, fella."

"I haven't any at the moment, but—"

"I put it on his bill, Mr. Fox," Mrs. Rabbit explained.

"Oh, no, you don't!" Freddie ordered. "No money, no honey. In fact," he said, shuffling through his notes, "let me see. Barnabas, Barnabas . . . Aha! According to my records, you already owe me for one cup of honey."

"Yes, I know, sir, but—"

"No buts about it." Freddie grabbed the elderly mole by the coat. "Pay up!"

"Mr. Fox!" Mrs. Rabbit protested. "Please don't shake him."

"Where'd you hide your money, mole? You've gotta pay up right now, Barny ol' buddy. Gimme this coat, and that cane, and let me have your hat."

"Mr. Fox!" Mrs. Rabbit pleaded.

"Another word," Freddie the Fox said, baring his sharp white fangs, "and you're fired, Mrs. Rabbit!"

"Please, Mr. Fox. Be patient," Barnabas begged, falling to his knees. "I promise to pay you back."

"I've heard that before," Freddie said. He started yelling, "Police! Police! This man won't pay his bill!"

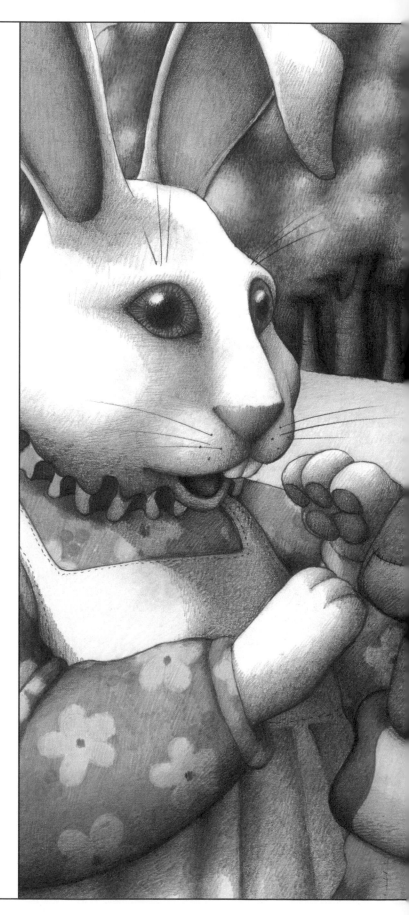

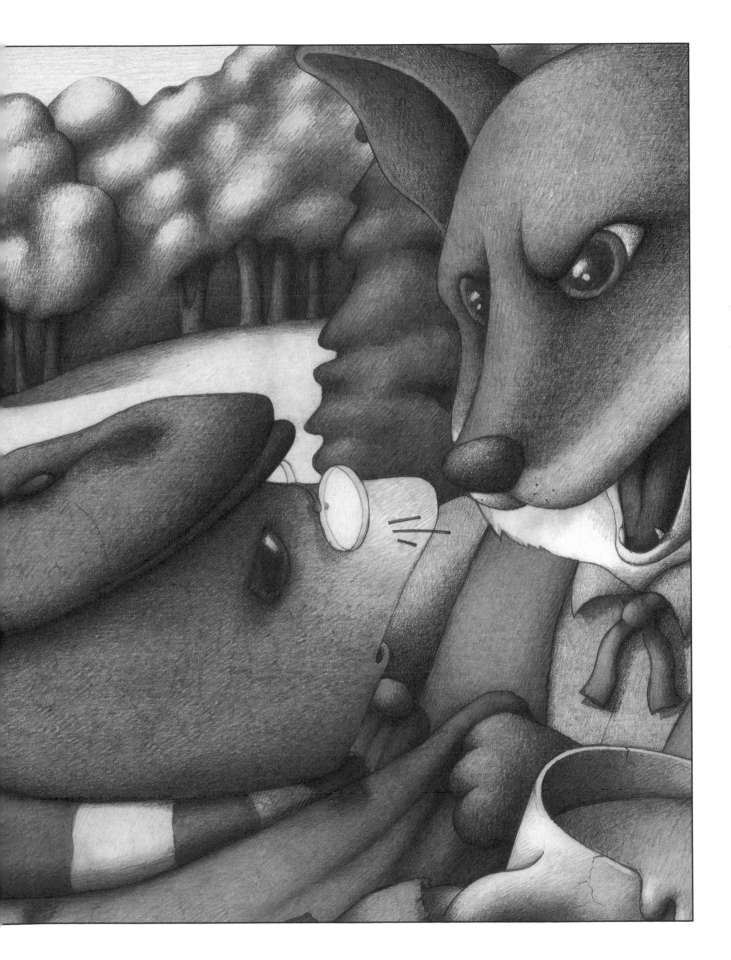

It took only moments for Freddie's shouts to reach the nearby police station, and before Mrs. Rabbit could think of a way to help poor old Barnabas, two badgers arrived in dark blue uniforms.

"What seems to be the problem here?" the first officer questioned.

"This bum won't pay his bill. He owes me for honey and claims he has no money."

"Well, sir, what do you have to say for yourself?" the second badger asked.

"I have no money," Barnabas answered, hanging his head.

"Sorry, fella," the first badger said, "we're gonna have to take you in."

"Oh, Barnabas, I'm so sorry!" Mrs. Rabbit wailed as the two officers led him away down the path toward the forest jail.

Freddie strutted off down the opposite path, humming a happy tune. Mrs. Rabbit glared at him. "I must help old Barnabas. And I know just what to do!"

She quickly closed down the honeystand and made her way to Sir Humphrey's luxurious home. Soon she was ushered into Sir Humphrey's parlor, where he was about to sip a hot cup of apple tea and munch a plateful of dark-brown honey muffins.

"Sir Humphrey! Sir Humphrey!" she shouted, hopping up and down. "Oh, it was terrible!"

"Mrs. Rabbit, calm yourself. What is the problem?"

"Oh, sir, it was terrible! He's so cruel! He has no heart, no heart at all, I tell you!" And Mrs. Rabbit told Sir Humphrey all about what had happened.

When she was done, there was a long silence. Then Sir Humphrey bared his huge white teeth and let out a long, deep growl. "Why, that ungrateful little fox! Reginald!! Reginald!!" he roared.

"Yes, sir," the butler replied, coming into the parlor.

"Have Freddie the Fox summoned at once!"

"Yes, sir."

"And have one of the maids take Mrs. Rabbit to the sitting room for a nice tea."

"Yes, sir."

"And I have some other instructions . . . "

Later, when Freddie the Fox arrived, he strutted into the parlor after Reginald had announced him. "Say there, Sir H. What's up? Got a problem I can help you iron out? Say, thanks again for overlooking that honey jar mix-up."

"Be quiet. You," Sir Humphrey pointed with his big paw, "are a worthless servant!"

"Huh?"

"First you steal from me. That's bad enough. But then you go and have a respectable mole thrown into prison."

"Oh, I got you. You mean that Barnabas. Listen, Sir H, he's a bum, always trying to get something for nothin'. I turned him over to the police. That's the last time he'll bother us."

"You should have forgiven him."

"Hey, he owed me!" Freddie objected.

"If that is your attitude, Freddie, I have no choice but to take action. If you cannot forgive this small debt, then neither will your debt be forgiven you."

"What?"

"Reginald!" Sir Humphrey roared.

"Sir?" the butler responded.

"Call the police!" he ordered.

"Very good, sir," Reginald replied before reaching over to ring a bell hanging near the doorway.

"The police!?" Freddie screeched. "What are you doing?"

"Freddie," Sir Humphrey explained, "you will be residing in the local jail until you pay back all the honey you owe me."

"But— but—" the fox stuttered, "you can't do that."

"Reginald, are my other guests here yet?"

"Yes, sir," the butler responded. "Shall I show them in?"

"Yes, Reginald," Sir Humphrey said with a smile. "Show them in."

"Very well, sir," the butler nodded, opening the door and inviting the waiting guests inside.

Freddie's eyes got big when he saw Barnabas walk in. "What's he doing here? How did he get out of jail so fast? And, hey, why aren't you at your honeystand?" Freddie asked as Mrs. Rabbit came in.

"They are here at my request," Sir Humphrey explained. "Mr. Barnabas will soon be managing one of my honeystands."

"What!?" Freddie said in amazement.

"What do you say to that, Mr. Barnabas?" Sir Humphrey asked.

"Why, I would be honored, sir," Barnabas replied politely.

"You'll be taking Mrs. Rabbit's place," the wealthy bear continued.

"But, sir . . . ?" Mrs. Rabbit whimpered.

"Mrs. Rabbit, you will be taking Mr. Fox's job as chief over all of my honeystand operations," he explained.

"Oh, thank you, Sir Humphrey!" Mrs. Rabbit gasped in delighted astonishment.

"What about me?" Freddie asked. "What am I going to do?"

"You, Mr. Fox, are going to jail," Sir Humphrey said flatly.

"You— you can't do this! You just can't!" Freddie protested.

Reginald opened the door. "Sir Humphrey, the law enforcement officers have arrived."

"This is he, officers," Sir Humphrey pointed. "Freddie the Fox."

"Haven't we seen you somewhere before, buddy?" one of the officers asked.

"Come along, Mr. Fox," the second officer said. He and the other officer grabbed Freddie by the scruff of his neck and carried him down the hallway and out the door toward the jail.

Sir Humphrey waited until the door was closed. "Now, Mrs. Rabbit and Mr. Barnabas, we had better discuss the details of your new positions. As you know, selling honey can be sticky business . . ."

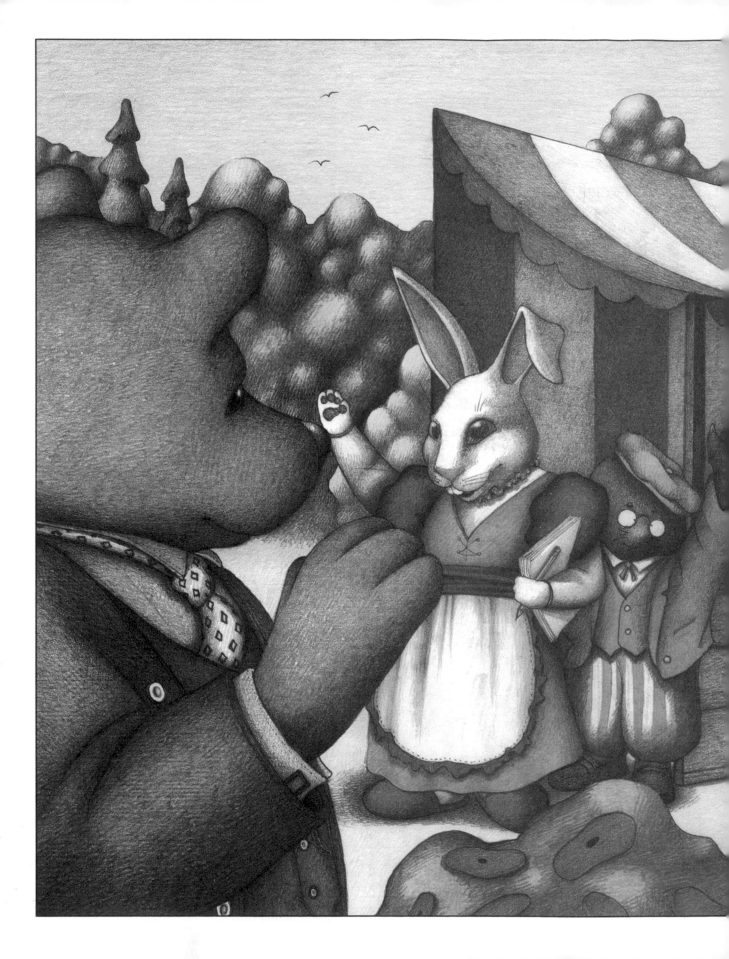

And so Sir Humphrey entrusted his honeystand business to Mrs. Rabbit and Barnabas the Mole. Barnabas soon became a skillful honey salesman, dealing fairly with all the forest animals. Mrs. Rabbit went on to do a splendid job of handling "Humphrey's Honeystands," keeping careful records on every jar of Sir Humphrey's honey.

With these two faithful servants handling his affairs, Sir Humphrey was free to spend his days lounging in his spacious mansion, sipping tea and eating muffins and honey.

As for Freddie the Fox, he became known as "the fox who wouldn't forgive." He remains in jail to this day, still paying back his debt to Sir Humphrey. He now has only 95½ jars of honey to go.

The End

You can read a story like this in the Bible. Jesus told it in Matthew 18:21-35:

Then Peter came to Jesus and asked, "Lord, how many times shall I forgive my brother when he sins against me?"

Jesus answered, "The kingdom of heaven is like a king who wanted to settle accounts with his servants. As he began the settlement, a man who owed him ten thousand talents [millions of dollars] was brought to him. Since he was not able to pay, the master ordered that he and his wife and his children and all that he had be sold to repay the debt.

"The servant fell on his knees before him. 'Be patient with me,' he begged, 'and I will pay you back everything.' The servant's master took pity on him, canceled the debt, and let him go.

"But when that servant went out, he found one of his fellow servants who owed him a hundred denarii [a few dollars]. He grabbed him and began to choke him. 'Pay back what you owe me!' he demanded.

"His fellow servant fell to his knees and begged him, 'Be patient with me, and I will pay you back.'

"But he refused. Instead, he went off and had the man thrown into prison until he could pay the debt. When the other servants saw what had happened, they were greatly distressed and went and told their master everything that had happened.

"Then the master called the servant in. 'You wicked servant,' he said, 'I canceled all that debt of yours because you begged me to. Shouldn't you have had mercy on your fellow servant just as I had on you?' In anger his master turned him over to the jailers to be tortured, until he should pay back all he owed.

"This is how my heavenly Father will treat each of you unless you forgive your brother from your heart."